THE PLANETARY SOCIETY

VENUS

EARTH'S TWIN

Bruce Betts, PhD

Lerner Publications ◆ Minneapolis

THE PLANETS AND MOONS IN OUR SOLAR SYSTEM ARE OUT OF THIS WORLD. Some are hotter than an oven, and some are much colder than a freezer. Some are small and rocky, while others are huge and mostly made of gas. As you explore these worlds, you'll discover giant canyons, active volcanoes, strange kinds of ice, storms bigger than Earth, and much more.

The Planetary Society® empowers people around the world to advance space science and exploration. On behalf of The Planetary Society®, including our tens of thousands of members, here's wishing you the joy of discovery.

Onward,

Bill Nye

Bill Nye
CEO, The Planetary Society®

TABLE OF CONTENTS

CHAPTER 1

EARTH'S TWIN

Venus is one of the eight planets in our solar system. They all circle the Sun. The Sun is the center of our solar system.

Venus is the second-closest planet to the Sun. But Venus is still millions of miles away from it.

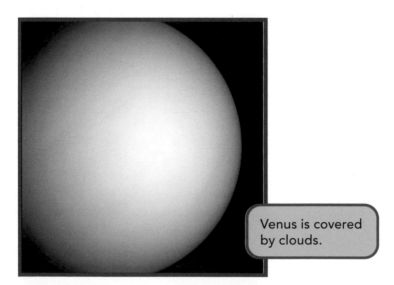

Venus is covered by clouds.

MEET VENUS

Venus is sometimes called Earth's twin. Venus is a little smaller than Earth. It is the closest planet to Earth.

VENUS FAST FACTS

Size	About 95 percent the width of Earth
Distance from the Sun	67 million miles (108 million km)
Length of day	About 117 Earth days
Length of year	About 225 Earth days
Number of moons	0

Earth and Venus have rocky surfaces. They both have an atmosphere. But Venus and Earth have very different temperatures.

Venus has the hottest surface in our solar system. It is much hotter than an oven! It can reach 900°F (482°C).

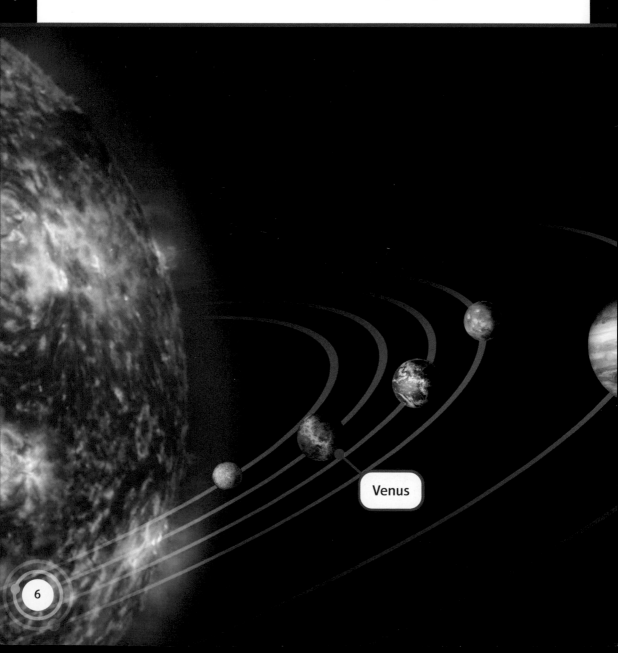

Venus

Mercury is the closest planet to the Sun. So why is Venus hotter? The answer is Venus's atmosphere.

The greenhouse effect is when gases in an atmosphere trap heat from the Sun. Venus has certain gases that make the effect stronger.

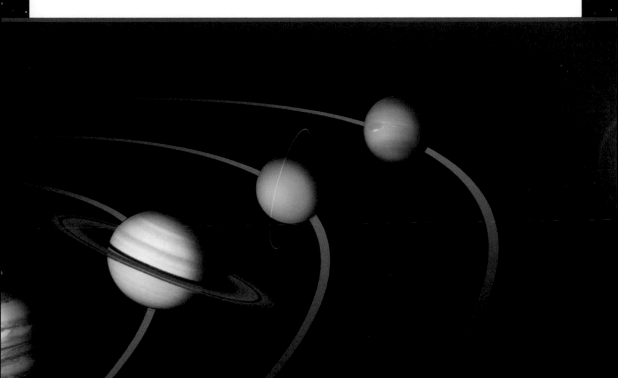

Clouds surround Venus. The clouds are made of a kind of acid.

Pressure is the force on an object. Venus has lots of pressure at the surface. It is caused by the weight of the thick atmosphere pushing down. You would not be able to stand on Venus because the pressure would crush you and the heat would burn you.

Soda on Venus?
The gas that makes up most of Venus's atmosphere is carbon dioxide. That is the same gas used to make the bubbles in soda.

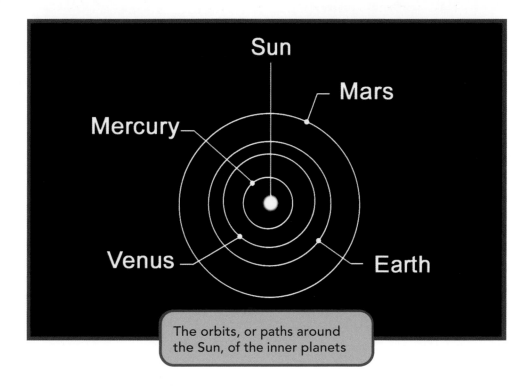

The orbits, or paths around the Sun, of the inner planets

One day on Earth is twenty-four hours. Venus spins much slower than Earth. One day on Venus is about 117 Earth days.

Venus rotates backward compared to Earth. The Sun rises in the west on Venus instead of in the east like on Earth. But if you were on Venus's surface, you wouldn't be able to see the Sun through the thick clouds.

A year is the time it takes a planet to go all the way around the Sun. One Earth year is about 365 days. One Venus year is about 225 Earth days. That means there are only about two Venus days in a Venus year!

MERCURY AND OTHER PLANETS

Venus is one of the four inner planets. Mercury, Earth, and Mars are the other three.

They are called the inner planets because they are the closest planets to the Sun. They are also called the rocky planets because they have rocky surfaces.

Left to right: Mercury, Venus, Earth, and Mars are the four inner planets.

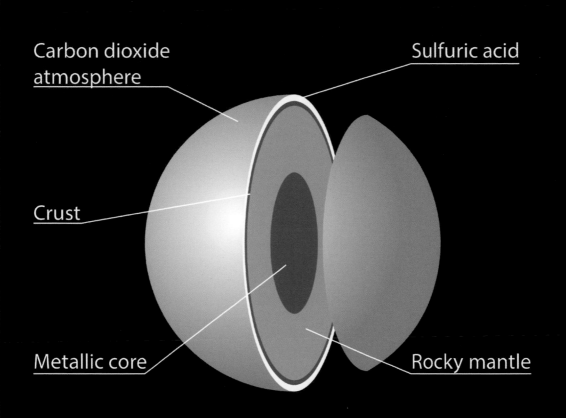

Carbon dioxide atmosphere

Sulfuric acid

Crust

Metallic core

Rocky mantle

Venus's inner layers

The inner planets have metal cores. When the planets formed, they were sometimes liquid. Iron and other metals sank toward the middle and formed the planets' cores.

CHAPTER 2

CLOUDY PLANET

Galileo used one of the first telescopes to watch Venus in the early 1600s. He saw Venus had phases. It was part of his proof that the Sun was the center of our solar system.

Our telescopes have gotten much better. We use them to look closer at Venus. Venus goes through phases as Earth's Moon does. As it goes around the Sun, we see different amounts of the day side and night side.

Galileo's drawing of the phases of Venus

Sometimes you can see Venus in the sky with just your eyes. It is much brighter than any star except the Sun. It looks so bright because it is the closest planet to Earth and is covered in bright clouds.

We can see Venus in the morning or evening sky. Many people thought it was two different stars. They called it the morning star or the evening star.

Venus looks like a bright star in the night sky.

Clouds and Wind

Venus looks different from the other planets because it is covered in bright clouds. It looks kind of like a bright white ball. It reflects a lot of sunlight on the side of the planet facing the Sun.

Venus often looks bright because of its bright clouds.

Speedy Winds

There is little wind on Venus's surface but strong winds high in its atmosphere. The strong winds rotate much faster than Venus does. This is called super-rotation.

Spacecraft have tools that see types of light that we can't see. The tools allow us to see the shapes of the clouds on Venus. Then we can study Venus's winds and clouds.

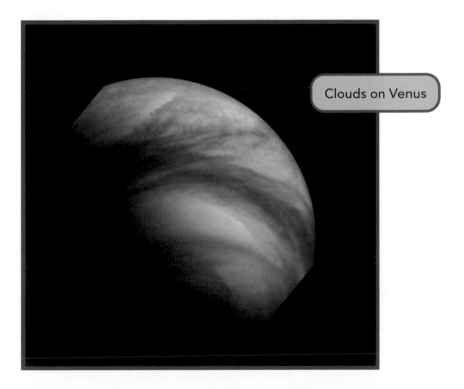

Clouds on Venus

Radar

We use radar to track where an object is and how fast it travels. One way people use radar on Earth is to see through clouds to track airplanes. We have also used radar to see Venus's surface through the clouds.

A collection of radar images showing one side of Venus

This image of the volcanoes Sapas Mons (*front*) and Maat Mons (*back*) was made with info from radar.

Venus has mountains, plains, and craters. Scientists have used radar to tell how high Venus's mountains are. Then they can create 3D pictures.

CHAPTER 3

EXPLORING VENUS

The planets are far away from Earth. Astronauts have not visited any of them. We use spacecraft to study the planets up close.

Scientists have sent more than forty spacecraft on missions

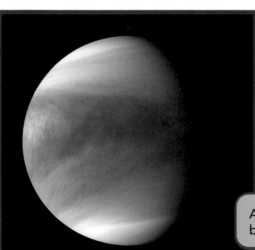

to explore Venus. Many of the missions have failed. But the successful missions have taught us more about Venus.

An image of Venus taken by a spacecraft in 2015

MISSIONS TO VENUS

Mariner 2 flew by Venus in 1962. It taught us about the hot surface, the atmosphere, and the clouds. It was the first successful spacecraft to explore another planet.

A drawing of Mariner 2

Some missions explored Venus's atmosphere. Many of them used parachutes to float down through the atmosphere. Then they all had parts melt from the heat or were crushed by the pressure.

Vega 1 and 2 left Earth in 1984. The balloons were made to fly high in the atmosphere where it isn't too hot. The winds blew them across Venus. They collected information about Venus until their batteries died after about two Earth days.

This is a model of a Vega balloon.

Magellan releasing from the Atlantis space shuttle to travel to Venus

Magellan reached Venus in 1990. It was the first spacecraft to take images of Venus's whole surface. It entered Venus's atmosphere and burned up in 1994.

LANDER IMAGES

Landers are a kind of spacecraft that lands on a planet or moon's surface. Venus's heat and pressure can crush or melt parts of landers. But some have made it to Venus's surface. They stopped working after one or two hours on the planet's surface when parts began to melt.

Four Venera landers have returned images of Venus's surface. The landers had cameras with fish-eye lenses. These allowed the cameras to see a big area.

Venera 9 and 10 sent back images in 1975. Venera 13 and 14 sent back images in 1982. The images showed lots of rocks and a yellow sky.

These pictures of Venus's surface were taken by the Venera 14 lander.

Tall Mountain

The highest mountain on Venus is Maxwell Montes. It's about 7 miles (11 km) tall. That is taller than Earth's Mount Everest.

KEY FINDINGS

Most of Venus is covered with volcanic plains. These flat areas formed when thin lava covered the surface.

Venus also has mountains and volcanoes. Venus has more volcanoes than any other planet. Most of them have not erupted for millions of years. We have found more than eighty-five thousand volcanoes on Venus. There could be more.

Earth has volcanoes such as this one, but Venus has many more.

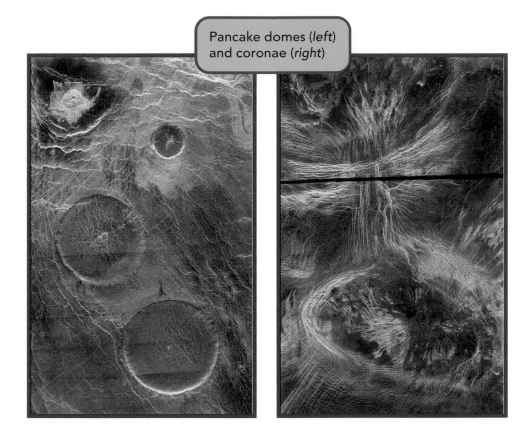

Pancake domes (*left*) and coronae (*right*)

Venus has pancake domes. They formed when lava spread out in a circle, or pancake shape. Coronae are only found on Venus. These landforms are hundreds of miles across and sort of round.

Some scientists think coronae might have formed when magma (molten rock under the ground) pushed up from below the ground. That would have made a big hill. The hill collapsed and lava leaked out.

Baltis Vallis is the longest known channel in our solar system. It formed on Venus by a thin lava flow instead of water flow. It is about 4,200 miles (6,800 km) long. That is a little longer than the Nile River!

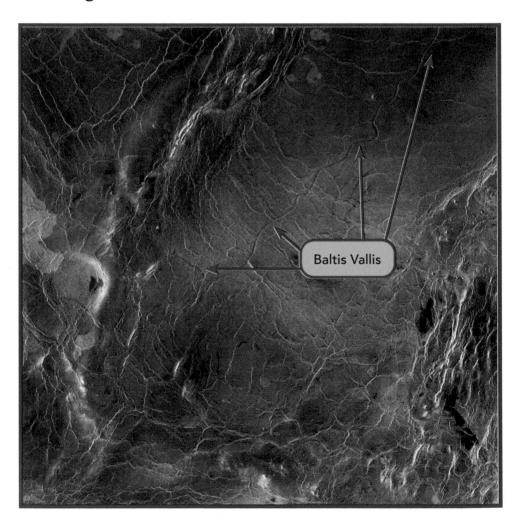

Baltis Vallis

Past and Future

Venus was very different in its past. Liquid water may have been on its surface. Now it is very dry and hot.

This artist's drawing shows what Venus may have looked like long ago.

You can look forward to finding out new things about Venus. More spacecraft will go to Venus in the future.

Venus is like Earth in many ways and different in others. By studying Venus and its history, we learn about the history of our solar system and Earth.

A model of the Venera 9 lander, which left Earth in 1975

The rocket launching with the Parker Solar Probe that flew by Venus on its way to the Sun

Glossary

acid: a substance that has lots of hydrogen ions. Strong acids can burn skin.

atmosphere: the gases surrounding a planet, moon, or other body

core: the center layer of a planet or moon

crater: a bowl-shaped hole caused by space rocks hitting the ground at high speeds

day: the time it takes a planet to spin around and go from noon to noon. One Earth day is about twenty-four hours long.

planet: a big, round, ball-shaped object that only goes around the Sun. Our solar system has eight planets. A planet does not have anything close to the same size near its orbit.

radar: bouncing a radio wave off an object and measuring what comes back. Radar can be used to see through clouds and to determine distance to the object.

spacecraft: a vehicle or object made for travel in outer space

year: the time it takes a planet to go all the way around the Sun. One Earth year is about 365 days.

Learn More

Bassier, Emma. *Venus*. Minneapolis: Cody Koala, 2021.

Betts, Bruce, PhD. *Earth: Our Home Planet*. Minneapolis: Lerner Publications, 2025.

Milroy, Liz. *Explore Venus*. Minneapolis: Lerner Publications, 2021.

NASA Space Place: All about Venus
https://spaceplace.nasa.gov/all-about-venus/en/

National Geographic Kids: Mission to Venus
https://kids.nationalgeographic.com/space/article/mission-to-venus

The Planetary Society: Venus, Earth's Twin Sister
https://www.planetary.org/worlds/Venus

INDEX

PHOTO ACKNOWLEDGMENTS

Images: F. Scott Schafer/The Planetary Society, p. 2; NASA/Johns Hopkins University/APL, p. 4; NASA/JPL, p. 6-7, 11), 14, 16, 17, 19, 25 (right), 25 (left), 26, 27; FoodAndPhoto/Shutterstock, p. 8; Betts/The Planetary Society, p. 9; NASA, p. 10, 27; Urutseg/Wikimedia Commons (CC BY-SA 3.0), p. 11 (top); Artwork by Galileo Galilei, courtesy of Wikimedia Commons, p. 12; Anton27/Shutterstock, p. 13; ESA/MPS/DLR/IDA, p. 15; © PLANET-C Project Team, p. 18; Geoffrey.landis/Wikimedia Commons (CC BY-SA 4.0), p. 20; NASA/JSC, p. 21; Russian Academy of Sciences/Ted Stryk/The Planetary Society, p. 22-23 (top), (bottom); Tatyana Druzhinina/Shutterstock, p. 24; Alexxx1979/Wikimedia Commons (CC BY-SA 4.0), p. 28; NASA/Bill Ingalls, p. 29. Design elements: Sergey Balakhnichev/Getty Images; Baac3nes/Getty Images; Elena Kryulena/Shutterstock; Anna Frajtova/Shutterstock. Cover: NASA.

FOR MY SONS, DANIEL AND KEVIN, AND FOR ALL THE MEMBERS OF THE PLANETARY SOCIETY®

Lerner Publications Company
An imprint of Lerner Publishing Group, Inc.
241 First Avenue North
Minneapolis, MN 55401 USA

For reading levels and more information, look up this title at www.lernerbooks.com.

Main body text set in Aptifer Sans LT Pro. Typeface provided by Linotype AG.

Editor: Brianna Kaiser **Designer:** Mary Ross

Library of Congress Cataloging-in-Publication Data

Names: Betts, Bruce (PhD), author.
Title: Venus : Earth's twin / Bruce Betts, PhD.
Description: Minneapolis, MN : Lerner Publications, [2025] | Series: Exploring our solar system with the Planetary Society | Includes bibliographical references and index. | Audience: Ages 7–10 | Audience: Grades 2–3 | Summary: "Why do some people think of Venus as Earth's twin? From surface temperatures to spacecraft exploration, readers will learn all about the hottest planet in our solar system"— Provided by publisher.
Identifiers: LCCN 2023038020 (print) | LCCN 2023038021 (ebook) | ISBN 9798765626825 (library binding) | ISBN 9798765628683 (paperback) | ISBN 9798765633441 (epub)
Subjects: LCSH: Venus (Planet)—Juvenile literature.
Classification: LCC QB621 .B425 2025 (print) | LCC QB621 (ebook) | DDC 523.42—dc23/eng/20231018

LC record available at https://lccn.loc.gov/2023038020
LC ebook record available at https://lccn.loc.gov/2023038021

Manufactured in the United States of America
1-1010098-52013-1/9/2024